PRESIDENTS' DAY

A TRUE BOOK®

by
Christin Ditchfield

Children's Press®

A Division of Scholastic Inc.

New York Toronto London Auckland Sydney
Mexico City New Delhi Hong Kong
Danbury, Connecticut

Reading Consultant
Nanci R. Vargus, Ed.D.
Assistant Professor
Literacy Education
University of Indianapolis
Indianapolis, IN

Content Consultant
Jonathan Riehl, J.D.
Writer, Congressional Quarterly
Washington, D.C.

A student drawing a picture
of Abraham Lincoln for
Presidents' Day

Library of Congress Cataloging-in-Publication Data

Ditchfield, Christin.
    Presidents' Day / by Christin Ditchfield.
        p. cm. — (A true book)
    Includes bibliographical references (p.) and index.
Contents: A national holiday — The Father of our Country — Honest Abe
— Ways to celebrate — Hail to the chief.
ISBN 0-516-22784-X (lib. bdg.)   0-516-27817-7 (pbk.)
1. Presidents' Day—Juvenile literature. 2. Washington, George,
1732–1799—Juvenile literature. 3. Lincoln, Abraham, 1809–1865—
Juvenile literature. 4. Presidents—United States—Juvenile literature.
[1. Presidents' Day. 2. Holidays.] I. Title. II. Series.
E176.8.D58 2003
394.261—dc21

                                                    2003004534

CHILDREN'S PRESS, and A TRUE BOOK®, and associated logos are
trademarks and or registered trademarks of Scholastic Library Publishing.
SCHOLASTIC and associated logos are trademarks and or registered
trademarks of Scholastic Inc.

1 2 3 4 5 6 7 8 9 10 R 12 11 10 09 08 07 06 05 04 03

Contents

Mount Rushmore, in South Dakota, is one of many monuments that honor United States presidents.

A National Holiday

On the third Monday in February, people in the United States celebrate Presidents' Day. It is a day to honor the country's leaders, especially George Washington and Abraham Lincoln.

George Washington was the first president of the United

George Washington (above) and Abraham Lincoln (right)

States. Americans call him the Father of His Country. Abraham Lincoln was the sixteenth president. He kept the United States from being torn apart during the Civil War. These men played very important roles in the history of the United States. People have found many ways to show respect for them.

Hundreds of books, plays, poems, and songs have been written about the lives of these two great presidents. Their pictures can even be found on

George Washington's face appears on the American dollar bill (above). Abraham Lincoln appears on the penny (right).

American money. George Washington's face appears on the quarter and the one-dollar bill. Abraham Lincoln's face appears on the penny and the five-dollar bill.

Many roads, bridges, rivers, schools, and cities have been named after these presidents. In the nation's **capital** city, Washington, D.C., people visit the Washington Monument and the Lincoln Memorial.

The Lincoln Memorial (above) and the Washington Monument (right)

These structures remind everyone of the wonderful ways these two presidents served their country.

Both of these famous presidents were born during the month of February. Americans used to celebrate their birthdays separately. Now they honor both men on Presidents' Day.

"The Father of His Country"

George Washington was born in the American colony of Virginia on February 22, 1732. As a young boy, George loved the outdoors. He enjoyed hunting, fishing, swimming, and horseback riding. He was tall and strong.

As a young man, Washington worked as a surveyor.

George wanted to be a soldier like his older brother. He dreamed of commanding a warship at sea. Instead, George became a **surveyor**. He learned how to measure land and make maps. When he was twenty-one years old, Washington joined the Virginia **militia**. He fought with British forces against the French to keep control of land in North America during the French and Indian War.

A Narrow Escape

As a soldier in the French and Indian War, George Washington faced many dangers and hardships. He risked his life to fight for his country. In one battle, he had a horse shot out from under him not just once, but twice! Four bullets ripped through his coat. Still, he rode back and forth across the front lines, giving instructions to his men. Amazingly, Washington was the only officer on the battlefield to escape unharmed that day. Every other officer was wounded or killed.

In 1759, Washington married Martha Custis. He lived a quiet life on his Mount Vernon **plantation**. Then, in 1775, the Revolutionary War began. People living in the American colonies were tired of obeying the British king. They believed the king's laws were unfair, and they wanted to govern themselves. They wanted to form their own **independent** country.

In 1775, leaders of the American colonies asked George Washington to lead the Continental Army.

George Washington was asked to lead the American forces, called the Continental Army, into battle against the British Army.

General Washington faced a difficult task. His tiny army was outnumbered from the beginning. The soldiers had little or no training. There were not enough supplies to feed and clothe them all. But George Washington loved liberty and was willing to fight for his beliefs. He inspired the men with his bravery. He refused to give up, no matter how bad things seemed. Washington's battle plans were very clever.

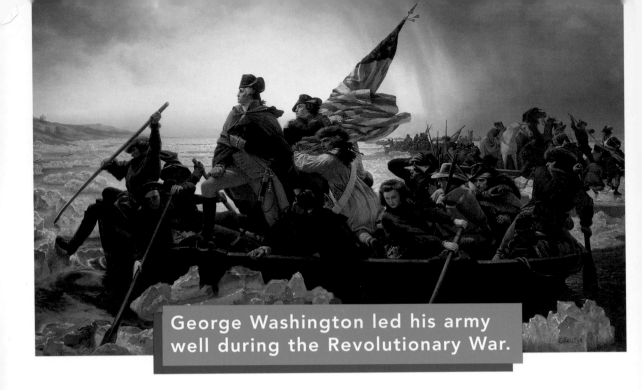

George Washington led his army well during the Revolutionary War.

He and his men outsmarted the British forces over and over again.

When the American colonies finally won their freedom, the new country needed a leader. George Washington had

become a beloved hero.
People respected his **wisdom**
and courage. They chose him
to be the first president of the
United States.

Crowds welcomed Washington when he arrived in New York to take the presidential oath of office in 1789.

Washington agreed to serve for two terms, or eight years. He knew it was important to set a good example for future presidents to follow.

Washington spent most of the rest of his life helping to shape the new nation. He died on December 14, 1799, at the age of sixty-seven.

It is often said that George Washington was "first in war, first in peace, and first in the hearts of his countrymen."

"Honest Abe"

Abraham Lincoln was born in a log cabin in Kentucky on February 12, 1809. Abe went to school for less than a year because he had to work to help his family. Legend has it that Abe taught himself how to read and write by studying the Bible—the only book his

parents owned. Abe loved to
learn. One of his neighbors out
on the frontier said, "He read

sitting, lying down, and walking in the streets—he was always reading." He was a kind, honest, and thoughtful young man.

Lincoln and his family moved to Illinois. He tried working at many different kinds of jobs. He worked as a sailor, a soldier, and a surveyor. He ran the post office and later opened his own store. Lincoln grew very interested in **politics** and law. He was a good speaker. People liked to listen to him

Several years before he became president, Lincoln took part in a famous series of debates about slavery.

talk about the issues of the day. Lincoln decided to study to be a lawyer. At the same time, he was elected to the Illinois State Assembly.

In 1842, Lincoln married Mary Todd. They had four sons.

Lincoln became a successful lawyer and a well-known leader in the community. He was elected to the United States House of Representatives in 1846. Abraham Lincoln became the sixteenth U.S. president in 1860.

Lincoln and his family during his presidency

"Dear Mr. Lincoln..."

During the presidential election of 1860, eleven-year-old Grace Bedell wrote a letter to Abraham Lincoln. She said that he should grow a beard. "You would look a great deal better for your face is so thin," she wrote. "All the ladies like whiskers and they would tease their husbands to vote for you." Lincoln listened to Grace's advice. By the time he was elected president, he had grown a full beard. He wore it from then on.

At this time, people who lived in the southern states depended on black slaves to run their farms and plantations. People in the northern states wanted to make slavery illegal. The question of slavery divided the country, like a house with a crack right down the middle. "I do not believe this nation can exist half slave and half free," Lincoln had said in a famous speech. "A house divided cannot stand."

President Lincoln believed that slavery was wrong. Still, the

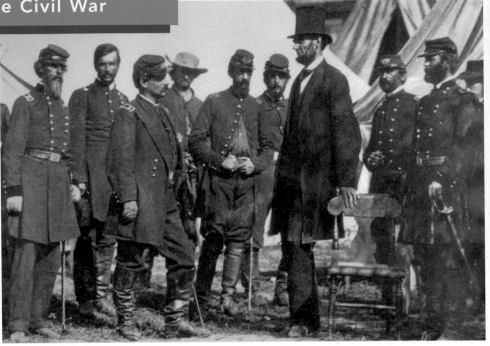

southern states insisted that it must be allowed. They wanted to withdraw from the United States and form their own country. War broke out between the North and the South.

During the war, President Lincoln signed a paper called the Emancipation Proclamation that gave slaves their freedom. He made sure that African-Americans, including former

President Lincoln reading the Emancipation Proclamation to members of his cabinet

slaves, were allowed to fight in the Northern Army. His wise and steady leadership helped the North win the Civil War. The United States remained one strong and united country.

Only a few days after the war ended, tragedy struck. On April 14, 1865, President Lincoln was shot and killed while attending a play at Ford's Theater. Millions of Americans **mourned** the loss of one of the nation's greatest presidents.

President Lincoln is carried out of
Ford's Theater after being shot.

Ways to Celebrate

During the month of February, schoolchildren learn all about George Washington and Abraham Lincoln. They read books that tell how these presidents served their country. Students act out historical plays and sing **patriotic** songs. They memorize some of the presidents' most famous speeches.

Schoolchildren learn all about Washington and Lincoln in preparation for Presidents' Day (above). Some students recite famous speeches by Washington or Lincoln (left).

The third Monday of the month is Presidents' Day. On this day, Americans take time to honor their country's leaders. All government offices, banks, and schools are closed for the holiday. Many businesses are closed, too. People celebrate with parties and picnics. They march in parades and attend memorial services to remember the presidents.

Actors dress up like George Washington or Abraham Lincoln. Large groups of people act out famous battles from the Revolutionary War and the Civil War. Some cities put on

Girl scouts watching a Presidents' Day parade (left) and people re-enacting a Revolutionary War battle on Presidents' Day (below)

special concerts and fireworks displays. Homes are decorated with American flags. Visitors place wreaths or flowers at the

has been elected, every American president takes the "oath of office." On the steps of the Capitol Building in Washington, D.C., he makes this promise:

"I do solemnly swear that I will faithfully execute the office of the president of the United States, and will, to the best of my ability, preserve, protect, and defend the **Constitution** of the United States."

Being president is not an easy job. The nation has many problems to solve. People have different ideas about what the president should do. He has to make difficult deci-sions, and sometimes people

A president must take command during a crisis. Franklin D. Roosevelt did this in 1941, when he asked Congress to declare war after Japan attacked Pearl Harbor.

disagree with his choices. A
president must work with the
lawmakers in **Congress** to
pass new laws that will keep
the nation safe and strong.

President Ronald Reagan
signing a bill into law

President Jimmy Carter brought the leaders of Israel and Egypt together to sign a peace treaty in 1978.

He meets with world leaders to establish peaceful relationships with other countries.

The president sets an example for all the citizens of the United States. In times of peace, he encourages Americans to follow their dreams and work hard to achieve their goals. In times of tragedy, he offers them comfort and support. In times of war, he takes command.

It is the president's job to offer people comfort and support after a tragedy such as a tornado.

Four former presidents (George Bush, Bill Clinton, Gerald R. Ford, and Jimmy Carter) and five former first ladies (Barbara Bush, Lady Bird Johnson, Hillary Clinton, Betty Ford, and Rosalyn Carter) at a presidential celebration

More than forty different men have held the office of president of the United States. In his own way, each one has done his best to serve the country. Presidents' Day is a day for Americans to say, "Thank you."

To Find Out More

Here are some additional resources to help you learn more about Presidents' Day:

 **Books**

Davis, Kenneth C. **Don't Know Much About the Presidents.** HarperCollins Publishers, 2002.

Harness, Cheryl. **Abe Lincoln Goes to Washington: 1837-1865.** National Geographic Society, 1997.

Harness, Cheryl. **George Washington.** National Geographic Society, 2000.

Sandler, Martin W. **Presidents: A Library of Congress Book.** HarperCollins Publishers, 1995.

St. George, Judith. **So You Want to Be President?** Philomel Books, 2000.

💡 Organizations and Online Sites

Abraham Lincoln's Birthplace
http://www.nps.gov/abli/index.htm

Take a virtual tour of Abraham Lincoln's birthplace in Kentucky. This site includes lots of photos and links to other sites about Lincoln.

Activities and Crafts for Presidents' Day
http://www.enchanted-learning.com/crafts/presidentsday

This site contains dozens of great craft ideas for kids.

The American Presidency
http://www.grolier.com/presidents/preshome.html

Grolier presents a history of presidents, the presidency, politics, and related subjects.

George Washington's Mount Vernon
http://www.mountvernon.org

Read all about the first U.S. president and his family. Tour his historic home and garden at Mount Vernon.

The White House
1600 Pennsylvania Avenue NW
Washington, D.C. 20500
http://www.whitehousekids.gov

Check out this site for photos and biographies of the presidents and first ladies, as well as games, quizzes, and White House trivia.

Important Words

capital center of a government

Congress members of the government who make laws in the United States

Constitution document that explains the rules for the American system of government and lists the rights of all American citizens

independent free; not controlled by others

militia group of citizens trained to fight as soldiers in an emergency

mourned felt grief about someone who died

patriotic expressing a love for one's country

plantation large farm where crops are grown

politics activities of those who control or seek to control the government

surveyor person who measures an area to make a map or plan of it

wisdom knowledge

Index

Meet the Author

Christin Ditchfield is an author and conference speaker, and is the host of the nationally syndicated radio program *Take It To Heart!* Her articles have been featured in magazines all over the world. A former elementary-school teacher, Christin has written more than twenty books for children on a wide range of topics, including sports, science, and history. She makes her home in Sarasota, Florida.